freedom

freedom
in Love
with Life and
Light

POETRY ~ MUSINGS ~ ART

Nitsa Marcandonatou

LIGHT PRESS
Ashland, Oregon

Cover image: *Flowering thistle.* Photograph. Meadows Canyon
Trail, Tilden Park. Berkeley, California. 2010.

Book design and publishing services:
Constance King Design

Editor: Cynthia Helen Beecher

Light Press
www.nitsamar.com

ISBN: 978-0-578-32046-5
Printed in USA

introduction

This Anthology has been in the making for
over thirty years. It came together during the
pandemic lockdowns of 2020. It is a labor of love
reflecting only one facet of Reality.

What is seemingly real is we are living in times
of great unrest and change. We are also living
in times of great opportunity ~ shining our
loving light and sharing it freely with
everyone and everything.

Tulip petals. Photograph. Boulder, Colorado. 2012.

"The more total you are, the deeper your relationship can be to any other human being. Once you find that inner core of yourself, you're free. And that leaves everyone around you free. You're not trying to make them into anything. You're not telling them what is best for them. You *know* you don't know that. What you're doing is receiving them fully as the human beings they are. This is where love begins; it sees the mystery of the other and is just overwhelmed by it."

The Feminine Face of God:
The Unfolding of the Sacred in Women

Sherry Ruth Anderson and Patricia Hopkins

"Love is what you are already. Love doesn't seek anything. It's already complete. It doesn't want, doesn't need, has no *shoulds*. It already has everything it wants, it already *is* everything it wants, just the way it wants it. So when I hear people say that they love someone and want to be loved in return, I know they're not talking about love. They're talking about something else."

I Need Your Love – Is That True?
How to Stop Seeking Love, Approval, and Appreciation
and Start Finding Them Instead

Byron Katie
with Michael Katz

"There is a vitality, a life force, an energy, a quickening that is translated through you into action, and because there is only one of you in all time, this expression is unique. And if you block it, it will never exist through any other medium and be lost. The world will not have it. It is not your business to determine how good it is nor how valuable nor how it compares with other expressions. It is your business to keep it yours clearly and directly, to keep the channel open."

Martha: The Life and Work of Martha Graham
A Biography
Agnes de Mille

"We ask ourselves, Who am I to be brilliant, gorgeous, talented, fabulous? Actually, who are you *not* to be?... Your playing small doesn't serve the world. There's nothing enlightened about shrinking so that other people won't feel insecure around you. We are all meant to shine, as children do... And as we let our own light shine, we unconsciously give other people permission to do the same. As we're liberated from our own fear, our presence automatically liberates others."

A Return to Love: Reflections on the Principles of
A Course in Miracles
Marianne Williamson

contents

Young Peregrine Falcon.
Photograph by Ulrich Roesch.

to falcon

for you

Living
Waters

Sages of Tuesday, September 17th, 2019

I

a.m.

the heart stood still
on this precipice of
a deep dark   secret

               unconditionally loved

                 seen and accepted

                    by another

shame became a watershed to   *freedom*

p.m.

marked the time
       at the Heartwater's source
              where love's floodgate shook and shattered

walking across
       holy Headwaters
              of the mighty Mississippi

washing away
       muddy deposits
              of a withered self ~

freedom it was
       stepping onto those
              smooth slippery stones

Two days later...

a.m.

As I crossed, the humble beginnings of the flowing one brought with it
Immense power of clarity and beauty stunning the mind to stillness
Melting this heart into meandering streams of exquisite tenderness

Where do I belong in this depth of connection with the grand old river?
My heart warm and watery cries out to it as if it's a close intimate beloved
Who are you? Where do you come from my love? What are you?

p.m.

Torrent teary rivers crest thresholds
    Of two new-born eyes

Carrying a clear
    Open hearted seeing

~ All Is Lovingly Held As One ~

The Heartwater's Source

I Am That

I Am

I

p.s.

Early morning   by a friend
         freed
Late afternoon   by a river

II

thoughts

used to come   go   incessantly

without any reason

and now?

thinking   just sailing by

with no content or traces of life

III

cleansings

The mind baffled
by this airy breath
of nothingness

floods its creased
heavy crevices

finding only clear movement
of bright crystalline light

reflected by the friendly river
rushing over its borders
eroding everything in sight

IV

Elegantly so

Filling these big brown eyes to the brim

Sitting on a plane looking earthwards
Witnessing this majestic river
Winding down wide wavy runs
Flashing its face upwards

Yes! Let's talk about elegance

V

water

The connection to my river
    has taken its own wanderings

where tears and river
    flow freely with endless ease

sliding down cracks
    of skin and earth

marking deep channels
    with windy furrows

speaking volumes of
    what has yet to come

VI

blessed

by a river and a friend ~

who would have imagined
an all-encompassing love

pouring sweet benedictions
on this rickety old woman

raising smiles to the sun
bowing down to the ground?

VII

who knows?

Walking down
        this path of life

Maybe you will feel
        how loveable you are

Maybe you get to know
        your own current calling

Flowing like a river
        to its source

VIII

Where Edges Meet Eternity

As our journeys unfold

    eventually we begin to notice

        existence no longer

           belongs to us

instead

                we the river

              belong to this

        ever-present open loving Awareness

              actually

           We Are That

Appendix. *The Journey* (pp. 129-136)

Musings

listen to the stirrings of the river in your veins

it is softly murmuring your beloved name

*

it flows   ~   it knows

its rounded folds
are nothing more

than its moving soul

*

surging downstream

living waters

hold the swiftness

of purging us clean

*

the fastest way

maybe is

the slower one

the ability to receive

is sometimes greater than

the ability to give

*

Quantum Physics asserts

the observer   *is*   *the observed*

we might want to pay attention to the word

is

it may be the key to our seeking

*

a single Dancer

taking the form

of all Dancers

dancing its Dance

So Let Life Dance You!

Life

Creation

Opening our sensuous mouth

uttering a single word

worlds are born

Opening our dazzling eyes   sharp ears

worlds stare   hum

back at us

Smelling   tasting   touching

myriad worlds manifest

their tantalizing flavors

Offering intimate possibilities

aligning our senses

with the true nature of everything

Words are medicine

Words

    needing to sound

        intelligently wise

            so interestingly refined

Words

    fabricating tales

        making us believe in

            what we are

Words

    kindly spoken

        unleash hearts

            from timeless bondage

Wondering

    what songs are we *singing?*

        what songs are we *listening to?*

Appendix. *The Alchemy of Letters and Words* (pp. 137-139)

a mystery revealed

Reveled in olden times we find

Muses   heroines   devils

The question always is

What is a *devil?*

Could we be so bold as to suggest

Is it a life well *lived?*

The backward spelling ~ opposite meaning of *devil?*

As for *evil?*

Is to *live* a life

In the *now*

A life we *now own*

A life we have already *won*

Our very *own!*

Inspired by the line, "Devil spelled backward is Lived" from Terry Tempest Williams's book, *When Women Were Birds: Fifty-Four Variations on Voice.* 2012. New York: Picador (p. 96).

p a i n

A weighty hole in the heart hurts

with an ever pressing wanting

waiting for the healing to take hold

staying with this

unbearable pain

tending it tenderly

it stroked

a note of holiness

in the heart of an empty hole

death

My friend's mother dying
hangs heavily on my mind

especially while I sit
next to her husband of sixty years
watching his sweetheart fade away

my only hope is

> seeing him once more
> with a glimmer in his eye
> strolling down these corridors
> of an assisted living house

he now calls home

suspended in no-man's land
as death makes its noble entrance
for the final act

I sense a sigh of release
seeping effortlessly
through her sleep

gathering around her

    holding hands
    moistening lips
    caressing forehead
    whispering loving words

she flutters her eyes

    a breath barely breathed

       and dies peacefully

          in her beloved's arms

yes and no

I

our souls are locked
in endless slow tides
of never ending cycles

YES   to   living
NO   to   living

what is this tyranny
gripping and seducing us
away from ourselves?

what is driving
that incessant struggle
between yes and no?

II

these two tricksters

play makeshift
hide and seek

surfing waves of mischief

leaving us treading
troubling torrent waters

III

untethered   they bring
        great relief

sometimes   *yes*
        sometimes   *no*

IV

so it goes ~
        when we think we know

something happens
        and we don't

V

in this specious swaying between
        known and unknown

ceaseless stories flow
        now we see   now we don't

24

Ode to Smoke

Oh! what beauty there is
on this breathless dizzy day
where everything appears
as an illusory haze

where everything is
floating like a dream
making me feel bathed
in a soft light of daze

all is as it should be
nothing to change
nothing to see through
only my gifted gaze

beaming like a laser
piercing my very being
opening me up onto
other ways of seeing

Joy

From that care-free place

    in my body

        I celebrate

full

    vast

        happy

singing

    dancing

        laughing

I love this life   mine

    this life of yours   this life of ours

        what's the difference anyway?

Musings

being human

loving joyful sad angry moved quiet soft depressed stubborn sincere
playful hurt content sincere confused clear stuck happy lost sensual
frustrated fulfilled excited sexy compulsive doubtful caring anxious
touched fearful judgmental bewildered tender withholding helpful
interested obsessive curious thoughtful...

these and many more may all be packed into a single day's span
we shouldn't be surprised how sometimes
we feel so crazed!

*

I find

what is lovingly accepted

is instantly released ~

I can also live with it forever in

p e a c e

*

respecting and attending

to a grief   is an act

of self-loving

~ so it is with joy

it looks like

a wound is healed

when its source is forgiven

*

got guilt?
ask the secret question
So What?

see how fast it evaporates
bringing a giggle
to your sweet face

got shame?
Chuckle!

the secret being
treating yourself kindly ~

so tread with confidence my friend
for it's written somewhere

wherever we are
whatever we are
whoever we are
however we are

we are perfectly fine

our own vitality is vital

for the fullness of a

valiant vibrant life

*

great teachings say ~
being unattached to
resisting   avoiding   longing   searching
we move with the river of life

calling all souls to communion

with what *is*

nothing more

nothing less

Aloneness

Flaming Gorge, Wyoming

Wandering in the middle of nowhere
    an expansive desertness
        opens up before me

with nobody in sight
    only billowing clouds coasting by
        I witness a most breathtaking sight

on one side
    heat waves weaving waywardly south
        saturate the air with strong sagebrush scents

on the other
    impressive sandstone buttes
        stand as sentinels to stillness

and way down there
    the deepest blue of waters
        reflects the bluest of skies

    saying *Howdy!*

to this lone and wondrous traveler
    who cannot help but smile big
        as happy as can be

The Vision Quest

I

sheer surprises
this birthday year

of sixty two ~
honoring it

in the desert wilderness
of my Vision Quest time

embodying fully
an inner wildness

embedded into
my very core

II

from this small cozy tent of mine
perched high atop a desert plateau

surrounded by steep Colorado peaks
I watch the world go by

dark clouds passing through
little insects buzzing around

lizards scurrying away
ants inching along

tangled movements
of intricate songs

filling the air
with exquisite silence

III

roaming aimlessly
on parched arid land

I find

I no longer know
anything anymore

IV

the bugs
incessant companions

the weather
capricious with thunderous heat

the fasting from
reading music phones clocks

the hunger
oh yes! the hunger

four solitary endless days
with no food

only water to sustain
this aging bundle of bones

V

through it all
little gems appear

scattered along
ancient dusty trails

the holy and the ordinary
are one and the same

VI

doing nothing
I drop into a fold of calm

discovering yet another secret

how I see is
all I need to know

VII

the ritual of the fourth day
is releasing into the sacred fire

any need for
love   appreciation   approval

revealing a final precious gift

this pure love I feel
is mine to freely give

VIII

as the day comes to a close
in quiet reverence

I watch the sunset

soaking up its
fleeting fading rays

IX

I turn around
warmly welcoming

the moon's full golden glow

and a solitary life
about to be told

tucked in

I

All alone now
time is my own

able to be in this
bittersweet place

where tears still flow

as ease of being
bit-by-bit grows ~

II

surrounded by the Sangre de Cristos
listening to Taizé's *Alleluia* album

in the company of plains
and ragged-edged mountains

I begin to unwind
one heartbeat at a time

   What happened?

         What happened?

               What happened?

III

Rilke talked about it
in time   he said

living one's life
will bare its fruits

the fervent question
haunting one forever

will be known   in time
in the throes of living

         a life

well-being

settling in

going deep

finding

peace

love

joy

Aloneness

I

wanting or needing
nothing more or
nothing less from anyone
or anything anymore
is bearing its fruits

II

in the beginning…

aloneness felt deadly
as if all air
was sucked out of
a small town house
I used to live in

I would walk
into a room
and the gloom
would become
a somber tomb

that's how death
made its appearance
crowding my shaky ground
on those numbing
lonesome days

III

muted despair cloaked

my every thought and limb

revealing my searing wound

IV

gradually   ever so subtly

something   somehow

started to shift

V

and the tomb became a womb

setting me free from the tomb of loneliness

unto the womb of aloneness

confusion

Do I take myself seriously

        or

do I take myself lightly?

which one to take to heart?
which one to walk on?
which one to mind?

the answer appeared unhindered
      early one morning

              as the Infinite I take myself seriously
            knowing it   sensing it   feeling it

                  is essential

            taking myself lightly however
             is walking into the world

       this *world*   with its *infinite*   *light-hearted* ways *one lone poppy*

at the tip of a stem
        brightly orange and all
                moves playfully

as soft breezes
        tenderly touch
                her delicate petals

no

        effort

                here

just being who she is
        one lone poppy
                in the breeze

morning salutations

Free to be

the one and only

the only one

waking up

alone

each morning

and happily saying

to absolutely everyone

GOOD MORNING!

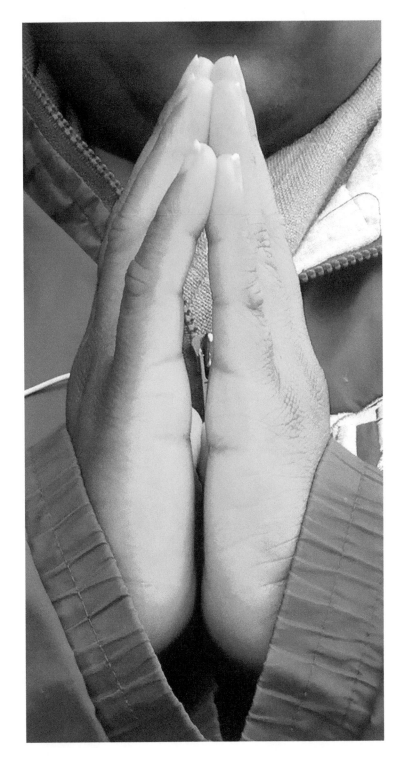

Musings

in our aloneness

we are one with all

we are al(l) one ~

at the same time

so utterly unique

*

loneliness   ~   aloneness

the power of surrendered acceptance

*

why do we want to be *the* one
when we are already that?

isn't being *the one* an inside job?
looking outside ourselves for *the one*

or

being *the* one in somebody else's life
may very well be a recipe for misery

*

reflecting on mind and matter
I find when it doesn't matter
and I don't mind
I fly free

to know is to be as the now

it is in the word itself

*

in the word know

is also the word   ~ no ~

so if we want to know

we get to choose

being in the

now or no(t)

*

now + here = nowhere = everywhere = Home

*

come closer than close to your wintry hollow
drink deeply

now is the time to know your own birth song
sing it out completely

Love

The Beloved

A teacher once said

    the beloved is just
    another sacred cow
     as all the others

       WHAT?

what are you trying to do?
take away everything from me?
isn't there anything I can behold anymore?

      N O T H I N G

holding Being in this way you said   I miss a

    simple
         ordinary
             breath
                 of who
                    I truly am

      it's a case of mistaken identity   you continued

         The Beloved

       we have been longing for
       has never been the other

    the other is only an~other expression of

        Being

       the truth is it's all about
       our heart's deepest desire

       to be the lover of Being
       The Beloved

     That We Are

embracing

Stripped fully of

    hopes and dreams

        especially all expectations

I am willing to be

    with you and me

        in this naked moment

open

    listening

        lovingly so

Love

cannot help itself but love

you and me

everyone

in every way

with the same

effortless grace

where all is illumined

from within

Be. Being.

Be   here   now

Being   here   now

one   an admonition

the other   a loving presence

hoping we are turning

into Being

unconditional love

When I heard

unconditional love

is not

unconditional license

my mind went stark blank

yet I knew

I needed to hear that

all I'm asking now

is courage

to speak the truth

dissolution

We want a beloved
    but we are afraid of intimacy

we want intimacy
    but we are afraid of merging

we want merging
    but we are afraid of commitment

we want commitment
    but we are afraid our beloved will devour us whole

well...
    we can count on it!

this is about so big a love
    it will obliterate us to smithereens

catapulting us *whole*
    into a whole new world

Blessings

Spoken through the grace of Debbie Crone
December 21, 1956 – June 8, 2021

I am one who lifts
into infinite possibilities
into the freedom of things

I bring you light-heartedness
and a deep sense of connection
with your beloved self

I am the one rising
from the depths of emotion
into the light of knowing

I bring you great blessings

may you be filled
with loving kindness
for yourself

and for all you touch with
your eyes your words
your smiles your hands

I bring you great loving

cherishing life

with all her inexhaustible treasures
  falling like sparkling jewels
    into my empty lap ~

blazing sunsets and burning sunrises
blinding snow on brazen plains
wreathing shimmery seas
high blue snowy mountains
long leisurely walks along misty coasts
falling leaves on cuddled cozy evenings
delicious lovemaking at the break of dawn

and oh! so much more...

if I had one word
  to cradle them all in
    it would be

      love

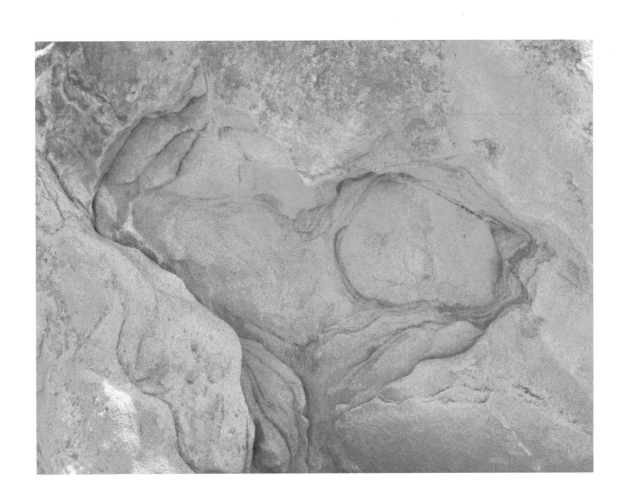

Musings

they tell you to be

considerate   patient   gentle   loving

are you?   to *you?*

*

as we set boundaries
we become stronger   bolder

a love
with no bounds

*

love and power

power and love

two consorts coiled at the core

*

We are the boundless blessings

All is well

love is the air we breathe

*

absolute honesty and being real

is what the heart really loves

absolutely

*

got inspiration?

go ahead
fall over heels
in love with it

any creative impulse
or intuitive urge
bursting through you

please

just do it

we all depend on it

*

just begin   the rest   will follow

Natural Beauty

Stillness

You have gone
to where I am going

so let me rest here
for a while

sensing you walking
into these lines   from time to time

(a tribute to Mary Oliver)

little insect

in one spot
      one speck
            so to speak

colorful
      dainty
            benediction

dangling gently
      from a tiny stem
            serenely still ~

suddenly
      she softly stirs

unfolds
      her luminous wings

and ever so lightly is
      taken by the winds

delights

At the outskirts of Crestone's high desert
        strolling along Willow Creek's cool shaded banks
                I suddenly stop   taking it all in

bright plump clouds
        traveling across
                dark imposing mountains

windblown ashen-branched aspens
        breaking a breathless spell
                that's all around

golden glimmering leaves
        cascading to the ground
                dancing their final airy pirouettes ~

such sunny blessings
        showering this willowy one
                blowing bubbly kisses to the creek

Sunshine Everywhere

Warmth   splendid sun drifts   quiet

And the Mind is Busy Trying to Find

Things to Do
Places to Go
New Country Roads to Roam

nothing wrong with all this   mind you
instead I stayed home in my tiny front yard

poppies blooming all around   little daisies happily showing their fresh
sweet faces   soft breezes smiling through me   tiny spiders spinning
their silky ways   bees buzzing along their endless merry-go-rounds
the ground tickled pink by the exuberance of Spring!

grey heron

A graceful grey heron
with her long
curvy neck

      poised

a solitary hunter
of long forgotten
haunting songs

her reflection on the lake
      a mirror image

of a dreamlike
      likeness

I take to be
      my very own

and the heart quivers
      regarding this fluid heron

a watchful regal guardian
      of ancient storied shores

gratitude

Curled up in bed

I quietly watch

a canopied camellia tree

coming alive as the cooling rain

moves through her glorious

green and red attire

sending shivers

up and down

her silvery spine

the Dodgeville cabin

In Dane County's countryside
    of aged rocky outcrops

there is this beauty
    of a cabin

nestled into the edges
    of dense woods

    imposing granite cliffs

    hover over swaying spent fields

    as critters meander leisurely by

here   life is

   simple

      easy

         peaceful

unwinding on the porch
    I lose myself

to the rhythms of a most
    exquisitely ordinary day

Beautiful Blue Butterfly

fluttery

        wispy

               whiffs

floating

      freely   D

        with   N

           the   I

                W

Musings

physical matter does matter   it's Infinity's density

it also doesn't matter

for the wise say   ~   we must die before we die

*

once in a while   let's just   *pause*

*

is the outer the utter manifestation of the inner?

*

the Big Bang could be Awareness's first booming sound

out of its stilled Silence

or

it could be Awareness's first creative dynamic impulse

of naming itself

I am

teachers keep telling us ~

what we look at   is what we get

but

how we see   sets us free

*

stumbling into a paradox

I fall right into truth

*

each day is brand new

it's just our minds

have not caught up with it yet!

*

beauty all around

nothing's missing in nature's

unbounded bounty

Light

eyes

only see what is swirling

in busy minds

while a solitary streak of light

burns right through brilliant bright sight

spilling out sparkly starry tunes

shape-shifting old stale tales of seeing

sitting and contemplating

The collage I have been working on
        throughout the day

suddenly comes to life
        shedding light to its own creation

a cutout circle
        with its emptiness

reveals no separation
        no distinction

one full
        the other empty

intersecting
        here and there

rendering their meaning
        here and there

all the while the fullness
        the emptiness

never leave each other
        they are always (t)here

sometimes empty   sometimes full
        sometimes intersecting

the question

"Speak to me."
"About what?" inquired silence.

"Oh, this and that."
"Then what?" asked silence.

"Just to know what I am
In this life of mine."

"Well," replied silence.
"In stillness

You are the light
My dreams are made of."

belonging

Longing to belong

in one way or another

finding that special safe spot

where my spark is

seen

held

accepted

respected

I sometimes wonder whether

belonging

is none other than the

longing to be

Fire

As the flame flickers

I come closer to you

whispering

your name

smiling faintly

you blow out the candle

and in the darkness

I finally know

my name

playful

radiant rays dance

through the air

as spectrums of light

play lightly with our hair

exclamation marks of

everything!   everywhere!

rainbows

Body settling on
      mossy decaying logs

resting at ease
      feasting on this tiny

color-filled
      ripple of a pond

as the day unfurls
      its priceless pearls

a baby fly
      lands on my page

iridescent beauty
      playing with my head

sun worshiper

Sunlight warming my back

filling my senses

to the brink

and I can't tell

whether my skin

is but a sunray's beam

Musings

have you ever considered
everything in the cosmos
is but pixels of light
each point refracting Consciousness
in seemingly multiple sights?

*

all's indivisible

except it's invisible

in an apparently visible universe

*

do you want to know who you *really* are?
sit quietly   take your time   ask sincerely

Who Am I?

the very moment you ask that question
you know

it is that simple

but the mind rushes in refuting anything
so *simply* revealed

my three-year-old grandson once said

the moon is God's flashlight!

he also said

I am empty of words

*

born of light   made of stardust

*

transcendence seekers

here is an axiom for us ~

in becoming immanent

being fully in our lively lovely bodies

transcendence becomes imminent

*

noseparationhere

*

there is this seamless movement of a ceaseless inner bowing

Pleasures

it's like this

One moment overtaken by bliss
      the next   overtaken by a cop
          with traffic ticket to boot!

     the difference is

first moment   extraordinary
second   quite ordinary

which one do you think
brings a smile to my face?

    the ordinary!
    you know why?

because now at each stop sign

     I brake completely

     take my sweet time

     breathe deeply

     and just like this

     fall right back

     into bliss!

fun

putting pen
      on paper
            letting it go

who knows what
will come out
on this virgin page

delight?
      insight?
           pain?

who knows?

letters

like droplets of dew on my tongue

I forge forth unto the unknown

a place where wild things slumber

the place of constant ebb and flow

that place where you are tongue-tied

as Mystery unfolds

r e l a x i n g

One other teacher said
the secret of life is to...

we all held our breath
riveted by the impending
revelation of great magnitude

        he continued
           relax

of course   *that's it!*
not only   *that's it?*

to any questions
we might have

all the answers
lie right here on this most
extravagant notion

coming of age

A seagull just landed

on my deck

and in front of me

an endless Pacific Ocean

glistening

ever changing...

it's my 65th birthday today

celebrating it

with gifts of

watery

windy

seagull

a moment

so surprising
    so splendid ~

a hot summer day
    wanders through the open windows

of this old comfortable
    on-the-road-again car

resting on top
    of barren rusty bluffs

looking out towards expansive plains
    back-dropped by the snow-capped Front Range

snowy peaks

Surrounded by glorious
    high mountains
        I am found in the middle
            of a pristine meadow

...breathing in
    frosty tingly sky
        my mind freezes
            in its heavenly tracks

Source

Heart   Earth

Each contains the other's holy letters

cuddled lovingly within them

a wholly whimsical world

Art

merciful

graceful

beautiful

Musings

we have framed ourselves
with flat edge-lined surfaces

while all along our bodies
are rounded curved sensualities

*

the problem is not all the thoughts we have
the problem is   I think!

thoughts have no center to spring from

when the center is established
all thoughts are a pleasure to behold

*

Being A Human Being

How Courageously Wonderful Is That?

*

c'mon   let's change things around our house

move stuff over to different places

loosen up   play a bit   have some fun

our dear home will definitely thank us!

illusions are precious

as they mirror precisely where we are

*

our dear   computers   smartphones   tablets

all related electronic gadgets

could we please leave them alone for a day?

they too need a break now and then!

*

slowing down   taking it easy

we have nothing to lose

but our dizzying minds

*

Holding your lover

Mmmmm...

Heaven!

freedom

secrets

I

one of the great secrets to freedom
which renders us

alive
engaged
spirited
awake

is the great fall ~

it's as inevitable
as the air we breathe

II

so let it rip my friend
for there's nothing to lose but our

notions
positions
judgments
beliefs

keeping us separately stuck ~
the secret to all this?   *f a i t h*

III

in this radical trusting time
we decide to follow
our own unique path

opening up to new vistas
of sweeping visions

leaving us all
hopelessly helpless
but of a different kind

IV

    without doing anything
        a surrendering starts stirring
            deep within us

    finding what was needed all along
        was our mere willingness
            to begin following

    the only path there is

        the pathless path

V

      allowing
    this mysterious path
      to unravel

    we get to where our path
      as well as others
        mix and mingle

    creating an inexplicable

      magnificent
      kaleidoscopic
      hologram

    of such intense beauty

    a hot flaming arrow
      fractures
    well-guarded shields

    exposing a tenderness
      of heart
    unto the welcoming light

fear

I

        doubt and panic
      spiral down the depths
       with no end in sight

       terror overtakes me

    as an insistent rehearsal
     suffocates and stutters
      the confused mind

II

did I just say

      the confused mind
        instead of
      my confused mind?

III

a flash of clarity
      shatters inextricable clouds
          of madness

as gratitude
      pours through
          feeling

relieved
    released
        remade

IV

I realize when
relief shows up

fear takes
the back door

and like a thief
gives itself up

V

but please let's not forget
        fear comes to visit us for a reason

an unfailing companion to our souls
        it's pushing us relentlessly

towards embracing the totality of our being
        bringing us intimately closer to the truth

VI

                when fear is

    understood   *fear has no power*

        felt   *fear has no hold*

        seen   *fear sets us free*

happiness

As more and more freedom
      seeps into my being
            the happier I feel

the happier I feel
      more and more freedom
            fills up my day

finding this
      fierce love
            living a human life

When

we are free we can
lovingly say to our
beloved

I don't need you
to make me
happy

and be in a most
intimate connection
forever

lockdown offerings

Being on a year-long retreat
I have been treated with a treat

finally finding the missing piece
I am no longer a child

no longer do I have to seek
no longer do I have to listen

to others' teachings of what to do and how to be
I no longer have to be present kind or real

I am present
I am kind

I am real
I simply am

Infinity

I

I start with
the infinity sign

moving my whole body
like a rhythmical
semi-circulous dance of

sensuality

pouring out
through pores
of this infinite body

where everything
speeding up
in standing stillness

is showing me silence
as its center
vibrating   electrifying

rendering the
Absolute   Obsolete

II

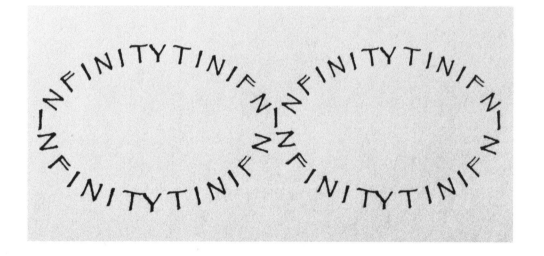

What the eye sees is the I of Infinity

I am Awareness

Resting as

                    A w a r e n e s s
        I n f i n i t e   E t e r n a l

I Am That

        I Am

                    names and words of power
                    for one loving name

                              I

            Awareness   Consciousness   Knowing   Silence
        Unknowable   Unnamable   Emptiness   Reality   Mystery
    The Absolute   Eternity   Infinity   Source   Freedom   Mother
Priceless Jewel   The Beloved   Heart   Mind   The Logos   All That Is
    Existence   Being   I Am   Light   Truth   Home   The Universe
    The Force   Divine Intelligence   Luminous Darkness   Essence
        Presence   True Nature   The Divine   Spirit   Life   Self
            Brahman   The Tao   Buddha Nature   Yahweh
                Goddess   God   Allah   Love   Peace
                    Happiness   Joy   Beauty

SILENCE

SILENCE

SILENCE

SILENCE

SILENCE

SILENCE

SILENCE

SILENCE

SOUNDING

SOURCE

SOUNDLY

116

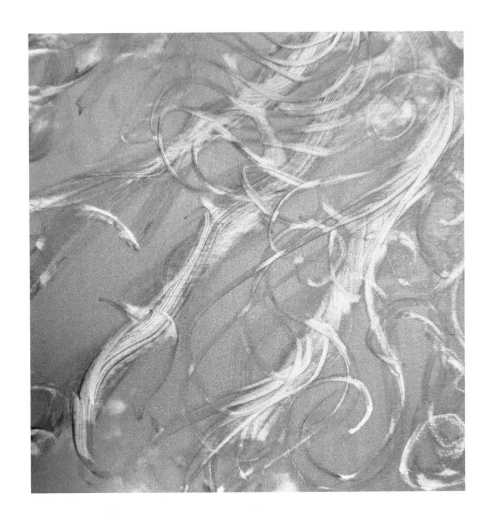

Musings

one of freedom's secrets ~

they say whatever we resist persists
so why not circle it in
to find out what it is?

*

having and making choices
does not mean I am in control

how about free will?
do I think I have that too?

I am told *reconsider*
as beliefs tend to be stumbling blocks

to my innermost
burning queries

*

Awareness does not reside

in the body or in the mind or in the world

rather

the bodymindworld resides in Awareness

~ not even that ~

All Is Awareness

As I stand in the center of the Labyrinth
These words come bubbling up

be still and know
I am
the human form

*

from the depths of our precious heart
comes a treasured trove of pure knowing
unsung by a human soul

*

Infinity infusing its affinity through a presumably finite
You

*

e m p t y i n g
more emptying

no end to this emptying
so it seems

*

I settle on this silent groundless
Ground of Being

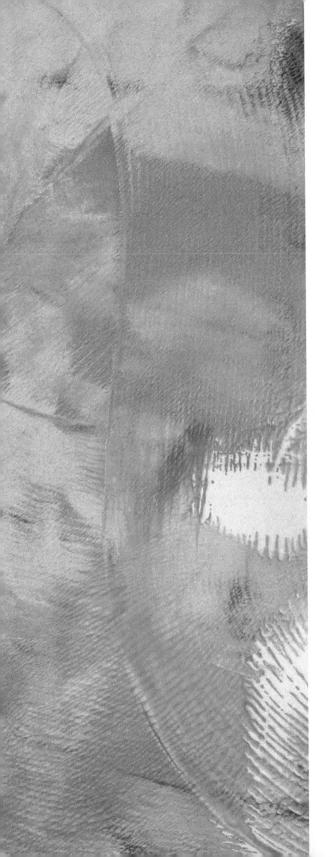

Conclusion

Freedom in Love with Life and Light

What I value the most
 where I hang out the most
  is Freedom

Such knowing required traveling over
 mountains and valleys
  with immense courage

Swimming upstream
 through raging storms
  of bitter tears

While all along
 this joyful aliveness
  kept shining its vibrant face

Revealing Freedom
 that tender
  loving space

Shifts

When we feel things are falling apart

maybe just maybe

instead

they are falling into place

a subtle shift in sensing

is all we need to feel at ease

Yes!

Living fully

with great faith

where all is offered up

to a mysterious movement

flowing swiftly through our soul

T o u c h e d

by a feather

flying

Free

Appendix

The Journey

In the early months of 2019, I was thinking of going on a seven-week road trip at the end of that summer. I wanted to connect with family and friends in California, Colorado, New Mexico, and Wisconsin. I also wanted to complete the last item on my bucket list – driving through the two remaining states of North Dakota and Montana.

As I was getting ready for the trip, I began having an intense premonition that I was going to die while I was on this journey. I explored those concerns with friends, inquiring and contemplating my fear of death.

A couple of weeks before leaving, my youngest daughter called to share she had dreamt that I had died. I was very alarmed, to say the least. At the time, she was not aware of my premonition. I told her about it. I also said that I had completed my will and if I were to die, I was mostly at peace with it.

I know now it was not about my physical death. It was a psychological death. It was also the death of four friends, unrelated to each other, who all died during the same week, two weeks into my trip. The incoming news was greatly disturbing, as two of those deaths were unexpected. Both had tragic endings. One of them had a profound influence on the *Living Waters* poems.

On August 8th, the journey began with a family reunion in Santa Rosa, California. It was a great gathering. We celebrated my grandson's transition into Middle School. I continued to Colorado visiting with friends, driving through the Rockies, relaxing in mineral springs, and paying respects at the great Stupa in Crestone.

My next stop was Albuquerque, New Mexico. I stayed with the first friend I made in this country when I arrived over fifty years ago. She lives in Old Town where she was born. Through her eyes I experienced the flavors of her town with its religious and spiritual aspects of indigenous cultures.

The drive from Albuquerque to Durango, Colorado was desert picture-perfect. I had a wonderful visit with my daughter and her husband in their new home. The drive from Durango to Moab, Utah proved to be even more memorable, as the La Sal Loop was breathtakingly gorgeous.

Before leaving for Wisconsin, I received an email from my friend with whom I was going to be staying. She gave me the horrific news that her seventeen-year-old grandson had been murdered a few weeks earlier. I spent a week with her and her husband processing his death, walking their pups, dining with family, visiting with friends, and driving with them around the beautiful countryside of Dane County.

There are these amazingly grounded and stable sensibilities in the mid-Western soul. People tend to put one foot in front of the other and do the best they can with what they have. There is no grand drama about anything, really. They deal with everything stoically. I have always admired these qualities of theirs, especially the enduring love they have for family, friends, and community.

On my last day with them, I asked if I could have their grandson's obituary. I placed it on the table in my room. That night I was unable to sleep partially because the energy of his obituary photo in contrast to his violent ending and my superstition that by keeping his picture while still on the road, might bring to pass my premonition of dying. Before dawn, I took the obituary into the living room and hid it under another one.

Early that morning, I left for Minnesota. When I arrived in Duluth, I texted my friend to say I had made it safely. I also thanked her for the warm hospitality I had received amidst their grief. I did not hear from her, so I began making up stories in my head that she had discovered the extra obituary and was extremely hurt that I had purposefully left mine behind.

During that whole day I was feeling guilty, but what I was really feeling was a sense of shame for the fearful and cowardly way I had acted. It was very painful to accept. I called her and left a voice message to please call me back. I went to bed exhausted, without hearing back.

The next morning, I saw she had texted me, *"Glad to hear from you. I know you will enjoy your journey home. It will be a journey of the heart... So glad we got to spend some time together during this time of grief and sadness for me. Drive safe sweetie! Nits, I tried calling as soon as I got your message. I'm so sorry I wasn't there for you. I'll call first thing in the morning..."*

When I read her message, I broke down crying. She did call that morning. I explained hiding the obituary and why, how I felt about my actions, and how sorry I was. In turn, she tried telling me not to be so hard on myself, that she understood. She also said I had to do what I needed to do to take care of myself, how much she loved me, and how much she appreciated my coming to be with her.

Throughout our conversation and me weeping with no end in sight, there was this palpable loving kindness coming from her that permeated my entire body, heart, and soul. That morning, on September 17th, I drove westwards through a torrential rain. It matched my unstoppable sobbing. Being loved, seen, and accepted unconditionally by another human being in all my humanity, was not only the biggest blessing I could receive, but it was also the most precious of gifts.

*

A few days before leaving Madison, a friend had mentioned that since I was driving through northern Minnesota, I would be close to the Mississippi River Headwaters. I looked it up on my phone and sure enough, it was about a half-hour's drive south off Hwy 2. That same afternoon I made the detour to see the headwaters.

As I entered Itasca State Park there was a large turtle in the middle of the road. I stopped to pick it up and put it out of harm's way, but something about it did not feel quite right. Its tail looked run over. Instead, I notified the Park Headquarters. They said someone would come by and move the turtle into the forest.

The entrance to the headwaters is located at the Mary Gibbs Mississippi Headwaters Center. At the beginning of the trail towards the headwaters there is a bronze sculpture of a woman created by Native American artist Jeff Savage titled, *Heartwaters ~ Caretaker Woman.*

There is a sign next to this beautiful sculpture saying that at the Headwaters of the Mississippi begin the Heartwaters of this nation.

In the Anishinaabe (Ojibwe) belief, women are the caretakers of the Water. Consequently, everyone needs to respect this responsibility of the sacred work of women by keeping this valued resource pristine and renewable for all future generations.

In the sculpture, the life force of the headwaters spills out of the woman's bowl (Lake Itasca), renewing the seasons and continuing the waters of life. She is holding a nest of turtles, which are strong symbols at this site. Turtles are believed to be important water symbols signifying the universal cycles of life. The woman and the turtles are placed on a drumhead. The drum represents the heartbeat of the Anishinaabe Nation, whose people believe their heartbeat is the true heartbeat of the water flowing from the heartland of this continent.

Lake Itasca ~ The Crossing ~ The Headwaters

At the headwaters, many people were wading in the river. A few were walking across a short path of large rocks, where the river begins flowing from Lake Itasca. These rocks mark the beginning of the Mississippi River, and it is known as "the crossing." The sign on the left says: "Here 1475 feet above the ocean the mighty Mississippi begins to flow on its winding way 2552 miles to the Gulf of Mexico."

The crossing is about twenty feet long and it is the only place where one can literally walk across the mighty Mississippi! I felt called to walk it. I took off my shoes, left them with my purse at the base of a tree, and began walking across.

The crossing was very slippery. I had to go down on my hands and knees a few times to stabilize myself. There were a couple of large flat colorful stones along the way. The water was crystal clear and cold. I reached the other side, took a deep breath, and turned around to cross back.

In the middle of retracing my steps, unexpectedly, my legs started shaking uncontrollably. I had to stand straight up to balance and gather myself. I looked out to the lake in sheer bewilderment. What had just happened? I had experienced this same energy surge once before, in the presence of one of my teachers.

When I went to pick up my purse and shoes, a gentleman approached me to let me know he had taken a picture of me walking across and wanted to know if he could send it to me. Now, whenever I look at that picture, I savor the crossing and the immense gratitude I hold in my heart for Mr. Richard Jackson of Minnesota who took the photo at the exact moment of my awe!

I thanked him and went for a hike around the lake to walk off some of the energy I was feeling. I needed to take in the peace and stillness of the place. The fall leaves were just beginning to turn a brilliant gold. The lake was calm. Solitude and beauty abounded. Everything was alive, vibrant, and somehow very soft. My heart was full. I felt baptized and blessed, yet again.

When I returned to the headwaters there was no one around. It felt auspicious to have the place to myself. I looked in my purse for a penny or a talisman of sorts. The only thing I could find was a small smooth rounded stone painted orange with red and blue flowers, and the word "free" written across the middle.

Four years prior, an artist friend had given me this beautiful stone and I had been carrying it with me all these years as a good luck charm. With heartfelt gratitude, I offered it to the Waters.

Leaving Itasca State Park, I drove west through North Dakota with its pristine prairies dotted with large refineries, shocking my sense of place. I stopped in Kalispell, Montana, where I spent two days to catch up with myself.

*

I continued south to Steens Mountain, a mountain range in the southeastern corner of Oregon, then went on a last exploration of the Frenchglen Loop, the highest road in Oregon, which crosses Steens Mountain peak. At almost 10,000 feet it stands out from the Alvord Desert and is only passable from July to October due to snow conditions. It is a spectacular fifty-nine-mile drive.

That last day, I stayed at Fields, an outpost with a two-room inn and one business, the Fields Station, with its own two-room motel established in 1881. It has two old gas pumps, a convenience store serving burgers and their world-famous chocolate milk shake. Absolutely delicious! It was exactly what I needed to celebrate the last night of my journey.

On September 23rd, I arrived home having driven seven thousand miles in seven weeks. When I parked the car, I hugged the steering wheel and wept.

*

A month later, I had to compose a poem for my elder women's poetry group. As I began writing about what happened on Tuesday, September 17th, to my great surprise, tears started flowing down my face. Twelve poems came streaming through. Eight are included in the *Living Waters* chapter.

I am still not sure exactly what took place on that September day. What remains is a sense of deep humility.

Epilogue

Since the first poem came through in October of 2019, I began tuning into the Mississippi River Headwater's webcam on a daily basis. I often teared up or smiled at the abundance of life that unfolded before me ~ from the summer visitors coming and going to the absolute stillness and stark beauty of the mid-winter wonderland, where a lone pileated woodpecker often frequented a certain tree branch as if to watch over the crossing.

For the entire year of 2020, every Monday at noon (CST), I took a screenshot of the headwaters. I also kept a daily journal of what I saw happening at the site. I am putting the photographs and notes into a large leather-bound journal and plan to offer it to the Mary Gibbs Mississippi Headwaters Center.

*

I'm still in wonderment of it all

What I do know is
My dearest friend is finding her way through her grief
My bucket list is fulfilled

And my love for the Heartwaters is steadfast
Checking the live stream regularly
Saying Hi! to my beloved friend

As life takes its twists and turns

I'm beginning to realize

The seven-week-long road trip was a

Pilgrimage

My good friend was right

When she wrote

"It will be a journey of the heart."

The Alchemy of Letters and Words

I have always been intrigued by words, especially by how letters come together to form words, and the way the mind has the freedom to create and use them to express, inform, educate, and entertain. For me, words have been my playmates and the playground upon which I let my imagination fly free.

I distinctly remember the first time I read about the Word. It was in St. John's Gospel in the New Testament. The first chapter begins with these words:

> "In the beginning was the Word,
> and the Word was with God,
> and the Word was God."

The Word, in its essential nature, is pure and sacred. Its sound creates worlds. My understanding of The Logos, the Greek translation for the Word, is that it is the creative expression of pure Consciousness or Awareness manifesting the World. The letter (l) in the word Logos is nested in the word World.

I continued reflecting on the usage of magical words and tools, which wizards employ in myths and fairy tales. A few of the magical implements they use are wands and brooms, usually made of wood crafted from a tree.

My reflections took me even further. I found that the image of the tree plays a pivotal role in most spiritual traditions. In mystical Jewish tradition, the Kabbalah, the tree of life, is central to its understanding of the sacred. In the Buddhist tradition, the tree under which the Buddha was awakened, also known as the Bodhi tree, signifies the tree of enlightenment. In the Judeo-Christian tradition, in the Old Testament, Eve ate the apple from the tree of knowledge. In the Islamic tradition, the tree is known as the tree of immortality.

At that point, I realized the above-mentioned trees could also personify Star War's tree of light. Interestingly, in our world, trees grow towards the light.

As I looked closer at these various words, I saw the letter (l) is part of the words life, enlightenment, knowledge, immortality, and light. In the word enlightenment, the word "light" is embedded in it. In the word knowledge, the letter (l) is nestled between "know" and "edge." And in my personal musings, I have come to understand that at the edge of all knowing there is only *Love*.

To love, one needs to listen deeply. The word "listen" is the anagram of the word "silent." So being silent, we listen, graced with the real knowledge of The Logos creating life and light through love.

The Logos

a word in a world   a world in a word

unto You

living a liberated luminous loving life!

then again...

words in our world

are like orphans

trying to create meaning of

~ what is ~

never quite making it

while all along

silence

ever so eloquently

beckons them back home

Art

Page 114   *Infinity*. Designed by Robin Rose (robinrosedigitaldreams.com). 2010.

Page 117   *Freedom to move*. Photograph. Enhanced by a q-tip dipped in alcohol. 8.5 x 11. 2015.

Page 120   *Flame*. Painting. Acrylic on paper. 8.5 x 11. 2015.

Page 126   *Moving bus* (detail). Photograph. New York City, New York. 2007.

Page 131   *Heartwaters~Caretaker Woman*. Photograph. Bronze sculpture by Jeff Savage. Mary Gibbs Mississippi Headwaters Center. Itasca State Park, Minnesota. September 17, 2019.

Page 132   *The crossing*. Photograph. The Mississippi River Headwaters. Itasca State Park, Minnesota. September 17, 2019.

Page 143   *Our earthly home*. Photograph. San Luis Valley. Hwy 17. Crestone, Colorado. 2016.

Page 149   *Author with Mt. Shasta*. Photograph by a visitor on Mt. Ashland, Oregon. 2019.

Gratitudes

My love goes to the four gems of this Anthology ~ Freedom, Love, Life, and Light. You are my cornerstones of Truth and Beauty bringing a sense of lightness into my everyday living. I thank you.

My everlasting love and great affection go to my loved deceased parents, Theano and Vassili Marcandonatos, the joys of my life, my grandchildren BenLuka and Sabine Sheddrick, my beloved and wise daughters, Alexandra Elite-Marcandonatou and son-in-law Aaron Sheddrick and Kristiana Elite and son-in-law Justin Elliott, my devoted siblings, Nicos Markantonatos and Aritsa Markantonatou and partner Yiannis Vardas, my good friend and father of our precious daughters, Tony Elite, and to my dearest Judy Borree and her dear family.

My heartfelt gratitude goes to Connie King, brilliant book designer and publisher extraordinaire. I could not have done this without you dearest Connie. I thank you so.

And to Cynthia Helen Beecher, my ingenious editor, who shaped the Anthology into a grounded and accessible piece of magic ~ my depth of gratitude has no bounds. Thank you so much.

With loving appreciation and a big bow to you my friends, my always-being-here close and dearest ones and to those who have touched my being, I thank you ~ Lori Ainsworth, Lori Almeida and family, Rena and Aleco Anastasiades, Sherry Anderson, Tomás Atencio and Consuelo Pacheco and family, Jan Augustus, Abatto Avilez and David Castiglioni, Giovanni Balduccini and Phillip Dudley, Len Barron, Ann Barton and family, Kim Bean and Jane Sadusky and families, Julia Bell, Jane Ngega Binagi, Bogus, Alexis Boufides, Avril and David Bright and family, Cricket and Jennifer Brooks, Eileen and Tim Bubniak and family, Carrie Callahan, Aurèle and Paul Carlat and family, Sue Carroll, Myrna Castaline, David Chadwick, Tamara Chan, Julie Connelly, Sheryl Cooke, Clare Cooley, Renée Côte, Eleanor Crescenzi, Debbie Crone, the Dalai Lama, Yiorgos Dalaras, Susanne Dane Lusk and Liz Lusk, Yiorgo Daskalaki, Claudia Debruyn, Fran DeGraff, Nan de Grove, Brenda DeVita,

Allie Dickson, Susan DuMond and Bob Armen, Yiannis Economides, Eeyore, Mary and Emmanuel Elite and family, Joyce Epstein, Doug Falkner, Norma and Reif Farris-Taylor, Barbara Findeisen, Margot and Don Fischer and family, Eleanor Flinn, Lea Flocchini, John Forsyth, John Francis, Fred, David Freeman, Meg Gaines and Margaret Mooney, Stephan Garbarino, Bernie Gardner, Murari and Prachi Garodia, David Gaskin and Phillip McPherson, Lois and Rudy Genetti, Peeter Gill, Beth Goldowitz, Paul Gowack, Joan Gray, Lawrence Greywolf and Alwine Goossens, Vern Haddick, Hafiz, Hal, Thich Nhat Hanh, Gregg Hansen, Maria and Andreas Hapsi and family, Peggy Heiner, Marilyn Hendee, Margot Henninger, Sister Henrita, Paul Herman, Denise and Steve Herzberg and family, David and Flo Hillard, Hannah Hinchman, Miriam Hobart, Sandra and Jim Hogue, Holling Clancey Holling, Patricia Hopkins, Bob and Donna Huntington and family, Christa and Bob Huseby, Wendy Hutton, Manabu Ikeda, Richard Jackson, Jen Jagielo, Jazzy, Ethel Jenson and family, Dave Johnson, Helen Kaprilian, Jan Karon, Byron Katie, Nikos Kazantzakis, Denise Kester, Peter Kingsley, Taylor Kohn, Helen and George Kostel and family, Danae Koumanakou, Fr. Nick and Presvytera Elaine Krommydas, k.d. lang, Stephanie Lash, Leigh Leibrook, John Leonard and Kenny Pennings, Lorrie LeSage, Martha Lewis, Maureen Longworth and Lin Davis, Sue Lopez, Elaina Lovejoy, Betty Lucatuorto, Nonia and Socrates Mamakos and family, Kathleen Manley, Toula Marcandonatou, Kathy Mattern, Heather Maxwell, Alexander McCall Smith, Tim McGraw, Becca McLennan and family, Deb Meyer, Patie and Rob Millen, Judy Miller, Cheri Milton, Nancy and Harrison Miner, Donna Morrissey, Anne Murray, Alan Neachell, Nellie, Mary Oliver, Trish and Tim O'Neil and family, Bill and Margaret Payne, Elizabeth Pelletier, Ken Pelletier, Naya Pennington, Kiara Perkins, Susanne Petermann, George Peters and Melanie Walker, Dave Peterson, Sylvia and Harry Peterson, Ioulia Pitsouli, Elizabeth and Merton Rapp, Terry Ray, Sarah Ritter, Chuck Roppel and Stefan Smith, Robin Rose, Francesca Rotondella, Tony Rubio, Rumi, Sue Sandson, Doug Schaeffer, Savannah Schedin, Tom and Nancy Schulenberg and family, Bev and Tim Schultz and family, Patricia Sempowich, Barb Settles and family, Sister Johanna Seubert, Jody Shevins, David Silverstein, Vernice Solimar, Joe Sonza-Novera, Noah Soulé, Gabrielle and Will Spencer, Larry Spiro, Mel Square, Sarah Stanke, Carol Stella, Anne Stine, Michelle Storm, Linda Sussman, Shunryu Suzuki Roshi, Sylvester, Rabindranath Tagore, Janet Tallman, Terry Tempest Williams, Kelly and Matt Thomas and family, Sylvia Timbers, Eckhart Tolle, Annie

Topham and family, Shirley Tremoulis, Kristen Tussey, Ron Valle, Marianna and Pavlina Veremi, Hugh Villalta, Lindsay Vineyard, Betty Warren, Donya Washington, Jeri and Graham Webster, Marybeth Webster, Lori Weiner, Taffy Wells, Jennifer Welwood, Maureen Wolf, and Marshal Zaslov.

My respect goes to all spiritual traditions and psychological teachings and their practices, which have contributed to my 'understanding' of inner and outer realms. Consequently, I want to thank my teachers Rupert Spira, Ellen Emmett, Karen Johnson, Hameed Ali, Carol Carbone, Adyashanti, Lama Pema, and Lama Yeshe. You have showed me ways of contemplating true nature in all its manifestations, especially...

... experiencing a deep personal enjoyment of the beauty, deliciousness and sacredness of its earth, sky, sun, moon, stars, the Orion constellation, cloudy and snowy days, rain, waters, birds and butterflies, redwood trees, flowers, shells, bones, heart rocks, lakes and reflections of any kind, rivers, wild wide open spaces, deserts, the African plains, the Pyramids, the Parthenon, the islands of Lemnos and Santorini, Matagorda, California, Colorado, Wisconsin, Oregon, the Indian and Pacific Oceans, the Aegean Sea and its beautiful beaches as well as Bowling Ball beach, Goat Rock beach, and Ocean beach in California, Mt. Tam, the Rockies, Mt. Shasta, Mt. McLaughlin, countless country roads I've roamed, trails, rituals, Vision Quests, music, poetry, art, SoulCollage, Casa Rubio B & B, I Am Harmony B & B, bicycles, books, bookstores where I have spent innumerable hours in, retreat centers, convents and monasteries, Labyrinths in Jenner, Petaluma, San Francisco, Madison, Sinsinawa, Boulder, Estes Park, Crestone, Ashland, Murphy, and Lincoln, Zoom and WhatsApp venues, yummy tastes of Greek and Thai foods, pomegranates, watermelon with feta, white ripe peaches, Candinas Chocolatier, tiramisu, crème brûlée, and so much more! Thank you for putting a happy smile to my face, bringing untold delights to my senses, and a restful fullness to my heart.

To the Mississippi River Heartwaters, I humbly bow to the power you hold to transform and wake a fathomless love for Waters, never before imagined.

To the beloved falcon, thank you for being a fierce companion in this life of mine. My deepest love and gratitude flow freely your way.

To you my dear reader
Holding the book in your hands
Is a great blessing to me
I thank you

Biography

Born and raised in East Africa 77 years ago, I was blessed to know big open skies, wide, wild places filled with animals, nightly sounds of drums and lions, and deep skies of brilliantly sparkled stars. Nature became my sanctuary, where to this day I find solace, solitude, and peace.

Living in Greece during my young adult years, I received the bounties of clear, crystalline light and transparent cerulean seas. Beauty became my muse!

Beauty has been a companion of mine since moving to the United States in my early twenties. I feel happy spending time in the wilderness, experiencing and taking photographs of detailed, stunning expressions of being.

My fascination with words comes from studying ancient Greek. It is interesting how, by combining letters we have the ability to form words, sentences, and paragraphs to exhibit distinct ways of seeing, understanding, and the making of meaning — especially through poetry. Writing poetry enriches my joy in life.

Art is a fairly recent discovery, having fun with all kinds of materials, including colored pencils, markers, aerosols, paints, pastels, images, fabric, and more. I am like a kid in a candy store marveling at the creative impulse that lies in each one of us, regardless of age.

At this point in my life, I am content and moved by cherishing family and friends, long solo road trips, having received a Ph.D. in East-West Psychology, teaching consciousness-based courses and workshops at a few universities and spiritual centers, volunteering at several hospices, at parks, and at public open spaces. Last but not least, I am content and moved by living on our beautiful and treasured planet.

My heart overflows with a profound love for goodness
and for the way Mystery keeps unfolding my life

CPSIA information can be obtained
at www.ICGtesting.com
Printed in the USA
BVHW090335310522
638487BV00020B/274